Chartered [...] and
illustrator [...] [...]ed up
to create a playful and uplifting guide
to positive thinking. Sam has spent many
years helping people take positive action
in their lives by making self-help strategies
engaging, practical and easy to use.

Read the psychologist's top tips and
integrate them into your successful life.

Enjoy the journey!

To:

With positive thoughts from:

Get Your Priorities Right!

If most of your time during the day is spent in crisis management and dealing with the urgent and important tasks, you should consider this: personal growth results from working on projects that aren't immediately pressing, but will bear fruit in the future. Fitness regimes, eating healthily and investing time in creative pursuits are all examples of positive investment activities.

Make time every day to work towards personal goals that will contribute to your brighter future.

What Is Important?

Sit down with paper and pen and ask yourself questions such as, "If I knew I couldn't fail what would I be doing?" and, "Who am I when I am at my best?"

Your answers will help you to discover your values and what is important to you in life. Set goals that reflect your values, otherwise your life will lose purpose!

Actions Not Outcomes

Setting goals is an important process as it helps to build purpose and discipline into your life. However getting too attached to achieving goals can be damaging to your day-to-day motivation.

Ensure that when you set a goal you identify the key processes and actions that you will need to achieve in order to succeed. Over thinking your goal will not help you achieve it but having a mindset that is focussed on action will work in your favour.

Accountability

Creating external pressure is a constructive way to help you succeed.

When you have set an important goal, create accountability by telling your friends and family about your plan.

The social pressure to deliver on your commitment will encourage you to be true to your word.

Stepping Stones

Think about the final
target of your goal and
then work backwards
to the present moment.

Identify the stages that you
will have to go through in order
to accomplish your goal.

This will help you to
construct a road map
and make the process
of reaching your goal
seem more realistic.

The Deadline

When you set your goals it is important that you give yourself a deadline.

Without a well defined end in mind you will lose focus and your goals and targets will drift.

When you reach your deadline, answer a simple question honestly, "Have I succeeded: yes or no?"

A Challenge Not A Chore

If you are going spend a lot of your time working towards your goal it is important to enjoy the journey.

Cherishing your progress and enjoying the challenge will also help you to stay motivated when you hit setbacks and unforeseen obstacles.

Visualise Success

The pictures and sounds that you make in your mind have a big impact on your behaviour. In your mind visualise yourself as you complete your goal. Add impact by making the picture big, bold and full of colour. Also notice how you will feel when you have reached you target. Feelings of pride, contentment and a sense of achievement will come to mind. The more you impress your mind with visions of success, the easier it will be to succeed.

Write It Down

Writing down your goals on the refrigerator, the desktop or stuck on the wall will keep them at the front of your mind. Filling your living space with reminders of your goals is vital because it creates a healthy pressure and helps you to streamline your focus and not become distracted.

The brain processes a lot of information that we are not consciously aware of, so visual reminders will be processed without your awareness and will support your progress towards your goals.

Bedtime Reminder

The brain is more receptive to suggestion just before you fall asleep. So before you drift off, close your eyes and imagine yourself completing your daily goals tomorrow with confidence and composure.

When you wake you will feel energised and motivated, ready to get going!

Be Ambitious

When you set goals it is important to be ambitious. It is better to set your sights too high and just miss out on hitting your target, rather than having a goal that is too easily reached.

The famous Italian renaissance painter, Michelangelo, said "The greater danger for most of us is not that our aim is too high and we miss it, but that it is too low and we hit it."

Go With Your Gut

Goal setting can be
a complex process.

Listen to your gut feeling
when you're unsure and hesitant.
Such instincts are an expression
of the unconscious mind.

This part of the mind can
size up your predicament
and make highly
effective decisions
very quickly.

Take Action

Any progress made in the world is the result of taking action. There is a danger that if you over-deliberate or procrastinate over a course of action, nothing will be achieved. Remember, "It is not the big that eat the small: it's the fast that eat the slow". (Jennings and Haughton)

Positive Framing

When you are setting goals make sure that they are focused on moving towards what you want, rather than away from what you want to avoid.
For example, the goal of getting out of debt is not as effective as the goal of becoming wealthier.
You get more of what you focus on, so if you are occupied with the goal of getting out of debt you will find even more debt to get out of!

Celebrate Milestones

When you start working actively towards your goals, it is important to celebrate your mini successes along the way. When you have devised an action plan specifying your roadmap, celebrate the small accomplishments as well as the large.

Completing a mini-target is a bit like passing a landmark that reminds you that you are on the right track. Making significant strides towards your goals should be rewarded with a well deserved treat.

Evaluate Progress

Actively working towards your goals can be a challenging process and it is likely that you will experience bumps along the way.

Get into the habit of evaluating your progress weekly. Write down three things that went well and three things that you aim to improve on in the following week.

This will help you to develop a balanced and constructive view towards goal setting.

Don't Try Too Hard

When you are determined to achieve your goals, it is natural to try too hard and so create tension that works against you.

Relax and aim for the middle ground between under-and over-reaching as you work towards your goals.

This will encourage you to progress with self-assurance and composure.

Positive Self-talk

We can influence the way
we feel by the voices we
generate in our minds.
Take advantage of
positive self-talk and
feed yourself with encouraging
suggestions. For example try saying
out loud or to yourself, "I feel
good and I am making progress
towards my goals". As long as it is
spoken with firm conviction,
whatever affirming phrase
you choose will have a positive
effect on your well-being.

Magical Momentum

Motivation levels suffer when our goals seem too large to achieve. When you set a goal, identify several simple actions that you can accomplish easily and immediately and start making progress.
The 17th Century scientist, Isaac Newton noted that, "An object at rest stays at rest and an object in motion stays in motion".
Take action, because if you start moving towards your goal it may become harder to stop than to keep going!

The Journey
Not The Destination!

You are going to spend most of your life working towards your goals and only a fraction of it will be spent on savouring your achievements.
Learn to cherish the journey as much, if not more than the destination.
This is where true happiness and self-fulfillment is found!

The Pocket Psychologist™
Other Titles in the Series

Published by Mindsport Ltd in 2012 - All rights reserved.
Printed in China

Mindsport Ltd
72 Prince Street, Bristol, BS1 4QD, United Kingdom
www.MyPositiveUniverse.com